The SUBTLE

ART

of CHOOSING YOU

Abrahm Turner

This book is a work of fiction and not intended to act in whole or part as the final authority on life's journey or to substitute for receiving mental health services.

Address all inquiries to:

Abrahm Turner

abrahmwrites@gmail.com

ISBN 978-0-578-38605-8

Printed in the United States of America

Houston, Texas 77011

About the Book

This book is a compilation of many occurrences during the high emotional phase of the author's life. Each day's affirmation reflects in part what came of that day. Please use the blank pages in between each entry to record your day. The author believes that any thought not recorded might as well not have been had.

Author's Notes

These blurbs include references to what the author was thinking, feeling, and experiencing while creating this work.

Personal Reflection

The sections are blank to record what you are thinking, feeling, and experiencing. The author hopes that this book will serve as a reminder of how you progressed and continued to thrive.

DAY 1

Every time you say no, you say yes to yourself in every situation.

_____

_____

_____

_____

_____

_____

_____

_____

_____

_____

_____

_____

_____

_____

_____

_____

_____

_____

_____

_____

_____

_____

DAY 2

The happiest you are often is a choice. Choose wisely.

DAY 2 Personal Reflection

DAY 2 Personal Reflection

Doodle your own inspiration

DAY 3

You are your most important asset.

Author's Note: Today was a hard day; how do you know when it's time to walk away? You have been here so many times before; why now? What makes this day so different? I never have the answers, only the perfect questions (Sigh)

_____

_____

_____

_____

_____

_____

_____

_____

_____

_____

_____

_____

_____

_____

_____

_____

_____

_____

_____

_____

_____

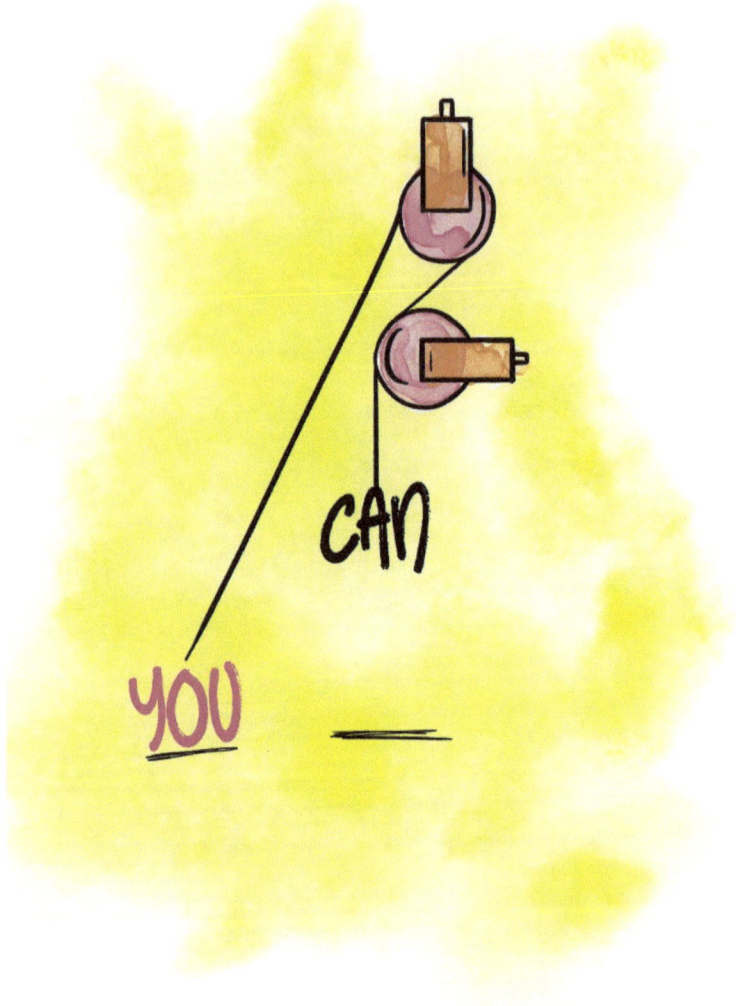

CAN

YOU

DAY 4

You control the levers to turn your liabilities into assets.

DAY 4 Personal Reflection

DAY 5

The recipe is perfect. You have equal parts mind, body, and soul.

DAY 5 Personal Reflection

DAY 5 Personal Reflection

DAY 6

Take time to sculpt the best you, even if that means starting anew.

Author's Note: So it's over, not because I wanted it to be but because it needed to be. You have to know you made the best decision you could, and you may come back to it, but for now, appreciate the memories.

_____

_____

_____

_____

_____

_____

_____

_____

_____

_____

_____

_____

_____

_____

_____

_____

_____

_____

_____

_____

_____

_____

_____

Doodle your own inspiration

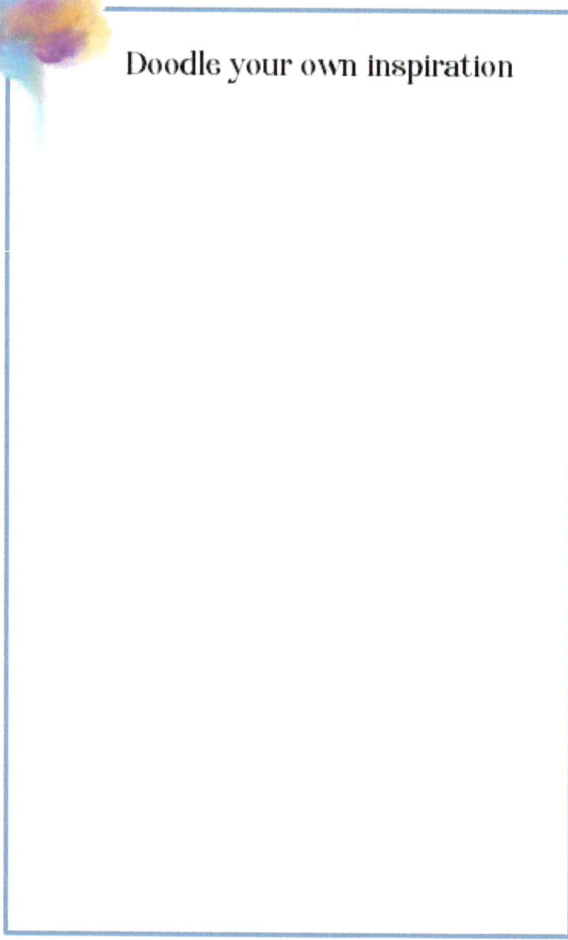

DAY 7

You are accounted for by simply showing up.

DAY 7 Personal Reflection

DAY 8

You within are more potent than you without.

DAY 8 Personal Reflection

_____

_____

_____

_____

_____

_____

_____

_____

_____

_____

_____

_____

_____

_____

_____

_____

_____

_____

_____

_____

_____

DAY 8 Personal Reflection

FREEDOM
IS
A CHOICE

DAY 9

To be free, you must choose to be free.

Author's Note: Here I go again, making the same choices repeatedly. When are we going to learn? Self-talk is crazy, but I might be a little left of the center today.

DAY 9 Personal Reflection

_____
_____
_____
_____
_____
_____
_____
_____
_____
_____
_____
_____
_____
_____
_____
_____
_____
_____
_____
_____
_____

DAY 10

Controlling you will not always be a cakewalk.

_____

_____

_____

_____

_____

_____

_____

_____

_____

_____

_____

_____

_____

_____

_____

_____

_____

_____

_____

Doodle your own inspiration

DAY 11

You have an immeasurable value.

DAY 11 Personal Reflection

DAY 11 Personal Reflection

DAY 12

You are always the best version of yourself at any given moment.

Author's Note: I got nothing. Just smile. Today is a good day.

_____

_____

_____

_____

_____

_____

_____

_____

_____

_____

_____

_____

_____

_____

_____

_____

_____

_____

_____

_____

_____

_____

_____

_____

_____

_____

_____

_____

_____

_____

_____

_____

_____

_____

_____

_____

_____

_____

_____

_____

_____

_____

_____

DAY 13

When you embrace yourself, the world will as well.

DAY 13 Personal Reflection

_____

_____

_____

_____

_____

_____

_____

_____

_____

_____

_____

_____

_____

_____

_____

_____

_____

_____

_____

_____

_____

_____

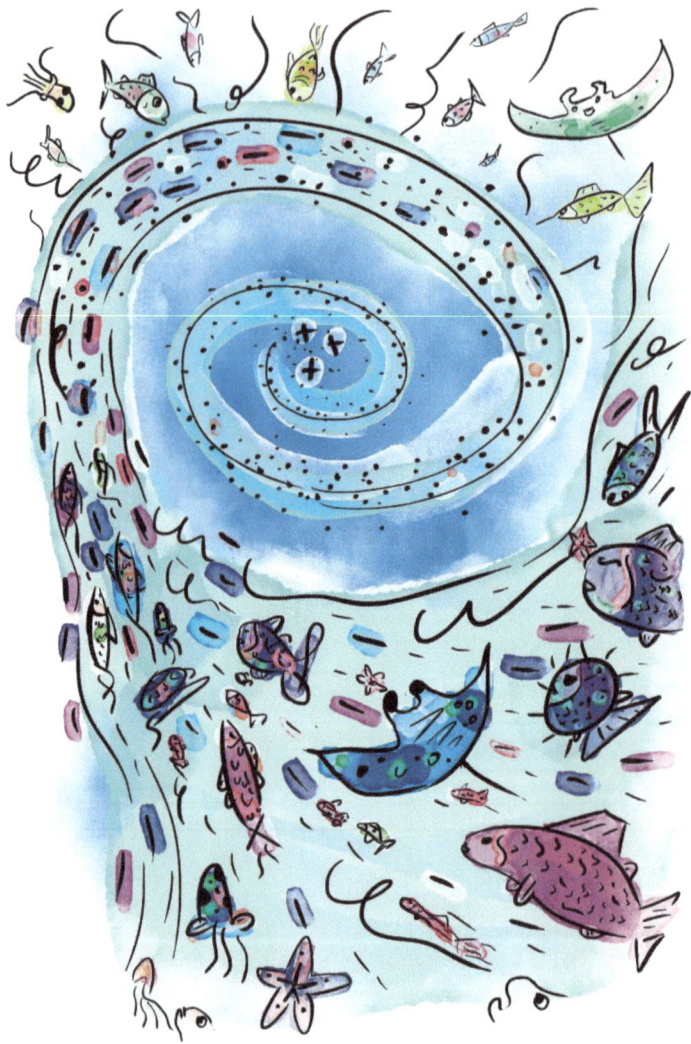

DAY 14

The authentic you will attract your authentic tribe.

Author's Note: I'm so tired of losing friends. This constant friend cycle is getting way old. Why can't people do the right thing? To think I'm the bad guy, Me?! You know they are lying, but why do so many people believe them?

DAY 14 Personal Reflection

DAY 14 Personal Reflection

Doodle your own inspiration

DAY 15

You deserve a break.

Author's Note: If you say to one more person that you are tired and do not take any PTO, whose fault is that? YOURS. You aren't being nice to yourself, are you? How will you fix your mouth to tell someone else how to care for themselves, and you neglect to take time when you know that you need it.

_____

_____

_____

_____

_____

_____

_____

_____

_____

_____

_____

_____

_____

_____

_____

_____

_____

_____

_____

_____

DAY 16

The first step you take toward anything is progress.

Author's Note: But what if I fail? You might fail, but let's do the math here; you have failed, but how many times did you succeed? That's what I thought. Go on head and get out of this bed.

_____

_____

_____

_____

_____

_____

_____

_____

_____

_____

_____

_____

_____

_____

_____

_____

_____

_____

_____

_____

_____

_____

_____

_____

_____

_____

_____

_____

_____

_____

_____

_____

_____

_____

_____

_____

_____

_____

_____

_____

_____

Doodle your own inspiration

DAY 17

Yup, it's on you.

DAY 17 Personal Reflection

_____
_____
_____
_____
_____
_____
_____
_____
_____
_____
_____
_____
_____
_____
_____
_____
_____
_____
_____
_____

DAY 17 Personal Reflection

_____

_____

_____

_____

_____

_____

_____

_____

_____

_____

_____

_____

_____

_____

_____

_____

_____

_____

_____

_____

_____

_____

_____

DAY 18

They are upset with you because you keep thriving. Apply pressure.

Author's Note: What is an imposter? Not you. Not ever. I have busted my tail to be able to sit at these tables and have these discussions. Carry on; they are just jealous.

DAY 18 Personal Reflection

DAY 19

You are the collection of your deepest thoughts.
Think and then become.

Author's Note: I know better than to be thinking like that.
Get out of your head and into your heart for once. Feel your
way through this. Call your friends; you need them.

DAY 19 Personal Reflection

_____

_____

_____

_____

_____

_____

_____

_____

_____

_____

_____

_____

_____

_____

_____

_____

_____

_____

_____

_____

DAY 20

You give, you receive. You lead by serving others.

_____

_____

_____

_____

_____

_____

_____

_____

_____

_____

_____

_____

_____

_____

_____

_____

_____

_____

_____

_____

_____

_____

_____

_____

_____

_____

_____

_____

_____

_____

_____

_____

_____

_____

_____

_____

_____

_____

Doodle your own inspiration

DAY 21

Your living is better than you just existing.

_____

_____

_____

_____

_____

_____

_____

_____

_____

_____

_____

_____

_____

_____

_____

_____

_____

_____

_____

_____

_____

DAY 21 Personal Reflection

_____

_____

_____

_____

_____

_____

_____

_____

_____

_____

_____

_____

_____

_____

_____

_____

_____

_____

_____

_____

_____

_____

DAY 22

Do more of what you love, less of what you don't.

Author's Note: Take the trip; you need this more than you know.

_____

_____

_____

_____

_____

_____

_____

_____

_____

_____

_____

_____

_____

_____

_____

_____

_____

_____

_____

_____

_____

_____

_____

_____

_____

_____

_____

_____

_____

_____

_____

_____

_____

_____

_____

_____

_____

_____

_____

_____

_____

_____

Doodle your own inspiration

DAY 23

You are more valuable than your paycheck.

Author's Note: I'm tired, BOSS; stuck between a rock and an even harder place. I'm tired of choosing between work and school, honestly.

_____

_____

_____

_____

_____

_____

_____

_____

_____

_____

_____

_____

_____

_____

_____

_____

_____

_____

_____

_____

_____

_____

DAY 24

For you, self-care probably looks like not just saying no, but &$!! NO!

_____

_____

_____

_____

_____

_____

_____

_____

_____

_____

_____

_____

_____

_____

_____

_____

_____

_____

_____

_____

_____

_____

_____

_____

_____

_____

_____

_____

_____

_____

_____

_____

_____

_____

_____

_____

_____

_____

_____

_____

_____

_____

_____

_____

_____

DAY 25

You are both the path and barrier to your success.

_____

_____

_____

_____

_____

_____

_____

_____

_____

_____

_____

_____

_____

_____

_____

_____

_____

_____

_____

_____

_____

Doodle your own inspiration

DAY 26

You Matter.

Author's Note: I repeatedly tell myself that life's destination will be more suitable this time. But man, I keep making these off decisions, and I will get it right one day because I know better.

DAY 26 Personal Reflection

_____

_____

_____

_____

_____

_____

_____

_____

_____

_____

_____

_____

_____

_____

_____

_____

_____

_____

_____

_____

_____

DAY 26 Personal Reflection

DAY 27

Saying yes to life means saying no to things that subtract from it.

DAY 27 Personal Reflection

DAY 27 Personal Reflection

Doodle your own inspiration

DAY 28

Things will come, and things will go; however, you will always be.

Author's Note: Man, please, this ain't what I signed up for. Adulting sucks. I need a vacation ASAP. I think the world thinks this mess is over, folks outside, outside, and I am still scared.

_____

_____

_____

_____

_____

_____

_____

_____

_____

_____

_____

_____

_____

_____

_____

_____

_____

_____

_____

_____

DAY 28 Personal Reflection

DAY 29

Your character will be felt long after you leave the room. Make it worth the while.

DAY 29 Personal Reflection

_____

_____

_____

_____

_____

_____

_____

_____

_____

_____

_____

_____

_____

_____

_____

_____

_____

_____

_____

_____

_____

DAY 29 Personal Reflection

_____

_____

_____

_____

_____

_____

_____

_____

_____

_____

_____

_____

_____

_____

_____

_____

_____

_____

_____

_____

DAY 30

You will crawl at times and teach others to fly. You will fly and teach others to soar. You are the force.

Author's Note: Why do the toughest battles come when I feel the weakest? I cannot seem to catch a break, but every time you look back over your life, you know that success is just on the other side of this hill. Keep climbing.

DAY 30 Personal Reflection

_____

_____

_____

_____

_____

_____

_____

_____

_____

_____

_____

_____

_____

_____

_____

_____

_____

_____

_____

DAY 30 Personal Reflection

_____

_____

_____

_____

_____

_____

_____

_____

_____

_____

_____

_____

_____

_____

_____

_____

_____

_____

_____

_____

_____

Doodle your own inspiration

DAY 31

You are what you see in others... There's a Subtle
Art in Choosing You!

Author's Note: You have made it this far, do not stop, do not
quit. I know you know what this feels like. You are tired and
worried, but you owe yourself to continue pushing into a
new day.

_____

_____

_____

_____

_____

_____

_____

_____

_____

_____

_____

_____

_____

_____

_____

_____

_____

_____

_____

DAY 31 Personal Reflection

_____

_____

_____

_____

_____

_____

_____

_____

_____

_____

_____

_____

_____

_____

_____

_____

_____

_____

_____

_____

_____

_____

- FIN -

www.ingramcontent.com/pod-product-compliance
Lightning Source LLC
Chambersburg PA
CBHW041955090426
42811CB00013B/1501